CW00501840

QUICK & EASY RECIPES FOR

APPETIZERS

Tina Collins

Table of Contents

LET'S START COOKING

Crispy Tofu

Preparation time: 10 minutes cooking time: 15 minutes serve: 4

Ingredients:

- 15 oz extra-firm tofu, pressed and cut into cubes
- 1 tsp sesame oil
- 1 tbsp rice vinegar
- 2 tbsp soy sauce

Directions:

In a large bowl, mix together tofu, sesame oil, vinegar, and soy sauce. Let it sit for 15 minutes. Place the cooking tray in the air fryer basket. Line air fryer basket with parchment paper. Select Bake mode. Set time to 15 minutes and temperature 400 F then press START. The air fryer display will prompt you to ADD FOOD once the temperature is reached then place tofu onto the parchment paper in the air fryer basket. Stir halfway through. Serve and enjoy.

Mustard Brussels Sprout Chips

Prep + cook time: 25 minutes 2 servings

Ingredients

- ½ pound Brussels sprouts, cut into small pieces
- 1 teaspoon deli mustard
- 1 teaspoon sesame oil
- 1 teaspoon champagne vinegar
- ¼ teaspoon paprika
- ¼ teaspoon cayenne pepper Coarse
- sea salt and ground black pepper, to taste

Directions

Start by preheating your Air Fryer to 360 degrees F. Toss the Brussels sprouts with the other ingredients until well coated. Transfer the Brussels sprouts to the Air Fryer cooking basket. Cook the Brussels sprout chips in the preheated Air Fryer for about 20 minutes, shaking the basket every 6 to 7 minutes. Serve with your favorite sauce for dipping. Enjoy!

Avocado Fries with Chipotle Sauce

Prep + cook time: about 20 minutes 3 servings

Ingredients

- 2 tablespoons fresh lime juice
- 1 avocado, pitted, peeled, and sliced
- Pink Himalayan salt and ground white pepper, to taste
- ¼ cup flour
- 1 egg
- ½ cup breadcrumbs
- 1 chipotle chili in adobo sauce
- ¼ cup light mayonnaise
- ¼ cup plain Greek yogurt

Directions

Drizzle lime juice all over the avocado slices and set aside. Then, set up your breading station. Mix the salt, pepper, and all-purpose flour in a shallow dish. In a separate dish, whisk the egg. Finally, place your breadcrumbs in a third dish. Start by dredging the avocado slices in the flour mixture; then, dip them into the egg. Press the avocado slices into the breadcrumbs, coating evenly. Cook in the preheating Air Fryer at 380 degrees F for 11 minutes, shaking the cooking basket halfway through the cooking time. Meanwhile, blend the chipotle chili, mayo, and Greek yogurt in your food processor until the sauce is creamy and uniform. Serve the warm avocado slices with the sauce on the side. Enjoy!

Spinach Chips with Chili Yogurt Dip

Prep + cook time: 20 minutes 3 servings

Ingredients

- 3 cups fresh spinach leaves
- 1 tablespoon extra-virgin olive oil
- 1 teaspoon sea salt
- ½ teaspoon cayenne pepper
- 1 teaspoon garlic powder

Chili Yogurt Dip:

- ¼ cup yogurt
- 2 tablespoons mayonnaise
- ½ teaspoon chili powder

Directions

Toss the spinach leaves with the olive oil and seasonings. Bake in the preheated Air Fryer at 350 degrees F for 10 minutes, shaking the cooking basket occasionally. Bake until the edges brown, working in batches. In the meantime, make the sauce by whisking all ingredients in a mixing dish. Serve immediately.

Crunchy Roasted Pepitas

Prep + cook time: 20 minutes 4 servings

ingredients

- 2 cups fresh pumpkin seeds with shells
- 1 tablespoon olive oil
- 1 teaspoon sea salt
- 1 teaspoon ground coriander
- 1 teaspoon cayenne pepper

Directions

Toss the pumpkin seeds with the olive oil. Spread in an even layer in the Air Fryer basket; roast the seeds at 350 degrees F for 15 minutes, shaking the basket every 5 minutes. Immediately toss the seeds with the salt, coriander, salt, and cayenne pepper. Enjoy!

Loaded Tater Tot Bites

Prep + cook time: 20 minutes 6 servings

Ingredients

- 24 tater tots, frozen
- 1 cup Swiss cheese, grated
- 6 tablespoons Canadian bacon, cooked and chopped
- ¼ cup Ranch dressing

Directions

Spritz the silicone muffin cups with non-stick cooking spray. Now, press the tater tots down into each cup. Divide the cheese, bacon, and Ranch dressing between tater tot cups. Cook in the preheated Air Fryer at 395 degrees for 10 minutes. Serve in paper cake cups. Enjoy!

Classic Deviled Eggs

Prep + cook time: 20 minutes 3 servings

Ingredients

- 5 eggs
- 2 tablespoons mayonnaise
- 2 tablespoons sweet pickle relish
- Sea salt, to taste
- ½ teaspoon mixed peppercorns, crushed

Directions

Place the wire rack in the Air Fryer basket; lower the eggs onto the wire rack. Cook at 270 degrees F for 15 minutes. Transfer them to an ice-cold water bath to stop the cooking. Peel the eggs under cold running water; slice them into halves. Mash the egg yolks with the mayo, sweet pickle relish, and salt; spoon yolk mixture into egg whites.

Arrange on a nice serving platter and garnish with the mixed peppercorns. Enjoy!

Green Bean Fries

Preparation time: 10 minutes cooking time: 10 minutes serve: 6

Ingredients:

- 1 egg, lightly beaten
- 1 lb green beans, ends trimmed
- 1/2 cup parmesan cheese, grated
- 1/2 tsp garlic powder
- 1 cup almond flour
- 1 tbsp mayonnaise
- 1/2 tsp garlic salt

Directions:

In a shallow bowl, whisk together egg and mayonnaise. In a separate shallow bowl, mix together almond flour, parmesan cheese, garlic powder, and garlic salt. Place the cooking tray in the air fryer basket. Select Air Fry mode. Set time to 10 minutes and temperature 390 F then press START. Roll green beans in egg then coat with almond flour mixture. Spray breaded green beans with cooking spray. The air fryer display will prompt you to ADD FOOD once the temperature is reached then add breaded green beans in the air fryer basket. Turn beans halfway through. Serve and enjoy.

Quick & Delicious Biscuits

Preparation time: 10 minutes cooking time: 10 minutes serve: 5

Ingredients:

- 2 eggs
- 2 tbsp sour cream
- 2 tbsp butter, melted
- 1 cup cheddar cheese, shredded
- 1/2 tsp baking powder
- 1 cup almond flour
- 1/4 tsp pink Himalayan salt

Directions:

In a large bowl, mix together almond flour, cheddar cheese, baking powder, and salt until well combined. Add sour cream, butter, and egg and mix until a sticky batter is formed. Place the cooking tray in the air fryer basket. Place piece of parchment paper into the air fryer basket. Select Air Fry mode. Set time to 10 minutes and temperature 400 F then press START. The air fryer display will prompt you to ADD FOOD once the temperature is reached then drop 1/4 cup sized of batter onto the parchment paper in the air fryer basket. Serve and enjoy.

Air Fried Walnuts

Preparation time: 10 minutes cooking time: 5 minutes serve: 6

Ingredients:

- 2 cups walnuts
- 1 tsp olive oil
- 1/4 tsp garlic powder
- 1/4 tsp chili powder
- Pepper Salt

Directions:

Add walnuts, garlic powder, chili powder, oil, pepper, and salt into the bowl and toss well. Place the cooking tray in the air fryer basket. Line air fryer basket with parchment paper. Select Air Fry mode. Set time to 5 minutes and temperature 320 F then press START. The air fryer display will prompt you to ADD FOOD once the temperature is reached then place walnuts onto the parchment paper in the air fryer basket. Serve and enjoy.

Parmesan Brussels Sprouts

Preparation time: 10 minutes cooking time: 12 minutes serve: 4

Ingredients:

- 1 lb Brussels sprouts, cut stems and halved
- 1 1/2 tbsp olive oil
- 1/4 cup parmesan cheese, grated
- 1/4 tsp garlic powder
- 1/4 tsp onion powder
- Pepper Salt

Directions:

In a bowl, toss Brussels sprouts with oil, garlic powder, onion powder, pepper, and salt. Place the cooking tray in the air fryer basket. Line air fryer basket with parchment paper. Select Air Fry mode. Set time to 12 minutes and temperature 350 F then press START. The air fryer display will prompt you to ADD FOOD once the temperature is reached then spread brussels sprouts onto the parchment paper in the air fryer basket. Top with grated parmesan cheese and serve.

Stuffed Chicken Jalapenos

Preparation time: 10 minutes cooking time: 25 minutes serve: 12

Ingredients:

- 6 jalapenos, halved
- 1/2 cup chicken, cooked and shredded
- 1/4 tsp garlic powder
- 4 oz cream cheese
- 1/4 tsp dried oregano
- 1/4 cup green onion, sliced
- 1/4 cup Monterey jack cheese, shredded
- 1/4 tsp dried basil
- 1/4 tsp salt

Directions:

Mix all ingredients in a bowl except jalapenos. Spoon 1 tablespoon mixture into each jalapeno half. Place the cooking tray in the air fryer basket. Line air fryer basket with parchment paper. Select Bake mode. Set time to 25 minutes and temperature 390 F then press START. The air fryer display will prompt you to ADD FOOD once the temperature is reached then place jalapeno halves onto the parchment paper in the air fryer basket. Serve and enjoy.

Spinach Sausage Balls

Preparation time: 10 minutes cooking time: 20 minutes serve: 10

Ingredients:

- 1 egg
- 1/2 cup parmesan cheese, grated
- 1/2 cup mozzarella cheese, shredded
- 1 lb sausage
- 1 garlic clove, chopped
- 1/2 onion, chopped
- 1 cup spinach, chopped
- 1 tsp salt

Directions:

Add all ingredients in mixing bowl and mix until well combined. Make balls from the mixture. Place the cooking tray in the air fryer basket. Line air fryer basket with parchment paper. Select Bake mode. Set time to 20 minutes and temperature 400 F then press START. The air fryer display will prompt you to ADD FOOD once the temperature is reached then place sausage balls onto the parchment paper in the air fryer basket. Serve and enjoy.

Tasty Zucchini Chips

Preparation time: 10 minutes cooking time: 12 minutes serve: 3

Ingredients:

- 1 egg, lightly beaten
- 1 large zucchini, cut into slices
- 3 tbsp roasted pecans, chopped
- 3 tbsp almond flour
- 1 tbsp Bagel seasoning

Directions:

In a small bowl, add egg and whisk lightly. In a shallow dish, mix together almond flour, chopped pecans, and bagel seasoning. Dip zucchini slices into the egg then coat with almond flour mixture. Place the cooking tray in the air fryer basket. Place piece of parchment paper into the air fryer basket. Select Air Fry mode. Set time to 12 minutes and temperature 350 F then press START. The air fryer display will prompt you to ADD FOOD once the temperature is reached then place zucchini slices onto the parchment paper in the air fryer basket. Turn zucchini slices halfway through. Serve and enjoy.

Perfect Cauliflower Tots

Preparation time: 10 minutes cooking time: 12 minutes serve: 4

Ingredients:

- 1 large cauliflower head, cut into florets
- 3 tbsp hot sauce
- 1/4 cup butter, melted
- 2 tbsp arrowroot
- 1 tbsp olive oil

Directions:

Toss cauliflower florets with olive oil and coat with arrowroot. Place the cooking tray in the air fryer basket. Place piece of parchment paper into the air fryer basket. Select Air Fry mode. Set time to 6 minutes and temperature 380 F then press START. The air fryer display will prompt you to ADD FOOD once the temperature is reached then place cauliflower florets onto the parchment paper in the air fryer basket. Meanwhile, in a mixing bowl, mix together hot sauce and melted butter. Once cauliflower florets are done then transfer them into the sauce and toss well. Return cauliflower florets into the air fryer basket and air fry for 6 minutes more. Serve and enjoy.

Crispy Air Fried Pickles

Preparation time: 10 minutes cooking time: 6 minutes serve: 4

Ingredients:

- 1 egg, lightly beaten
- 1/3 cup almond flour
- 16 dill pickle slices
- 1/4 cup parmesan cheese, grated
- 1/2 cup pork rinds, crushed

Directions:

In a small bowl, add egg and whisk well. In a separate bowl, add the almond flour. In a shallow dish, mix together pork rinds and parmesan cheese. Dredge pickle slices in almond flour mixture then egg and finally coat with crushed pork rind mixture. Place the cooking tray in the air fryer basket. Place piece of parchment paper into the air fryer basket. Select Air Fry mode. Set time to 6 minutes and temperature 370 F then press START. The air fryer display will prompt you to ADD FOOD once the temperature is reached then place breaded pickle slices onto the parchment paper in the air fryer basket. Serve and enjoy.

Asiago Asparagus Fries

Preparation time: 10 minutes cooking time: 10 minutes serve: 4

Ingredients:

- 1 lb asparagus spears, trim & cut in half
- 2 tbsp mayonnaise
- 2 oz asiago cheese, grated

Directions:

Add grated cheese in a shallow dish. Add asparagus and mayonnaise into the mixing bowl and mix well. Coat asparagus spears with grated cheese. Place the cooking tray in the air fryer basket. Line air fryer basket with parchment paper. Select Air Fry mode. Set time to 10 minutes and temperature 380 F then press START. The air fryer display will prompt you to ADD FOOD once the temperature is reached then arrange asparagus spears onto the parchment paper in the air fryer basket. Serve and enjoy.

Crispy Air Fried Zucchini

Preparation time: 10 minutes cooking time: 15 minutes serve: 10

Ingredients:

- 1 medium zucchini, sliced thinly lengthwise
- 1/4 cup mayonnaise
- 1 garlic clove, crushed
- 1/2 cup parmesan cheese, grated
- 1 cup pork rinds, crushed

Directions:

In a shallow dish, mix together crushed pork rinds and grated cheese. In a mixing bowl, mix together zucchini slices, mayonnaise, and garlic. Coat each zucchini slice with crushed pork rind mixture. Place the cooking tray in the air fryer basket. Line air fryer basket with parchment paper. Select Air Fry mode. Set time to 15 minutes and temperature 350 F then press START. The air fryer display will prompt you to ADD FOOD once the temperature is reached then place breaded zucchini slices onto the parchment paper in the air fryer basket. Serve and enjoy.

Cheese Balls

Preparation time: 10 minutes cooking time: 12 minutes serve: 8

Ingredients:

- 2 eggs
- 1/2 tsp baking powder
- 1/2 cup almond flour
- 1/4 cup parmesan cheese, shredded
- 1/4 cup mozzarella cheese, shredded
- 1/2 cup cheddar cheese, shredded

Directions:

In a bowl, whisk eggs. Add remaining ingredients and mix until well combined. Divide mixture into 8 equal portions. Roll each portion into a ball. Place the cooking tray in the air fryer basket. Line air fryer basket with parchment paper. Select Bake mode. Set time to 12 minutes and temperature 400 F then press START. The air fryer display will prompt you to ADD FOOD once the temperature is reached then place cheese balls onto the parchment paper in the air fryer basket. Serve and enjoy.

Chicken Meatballs

Preparation time: 10 minutes cooking time: 10 minutes serve: 6

Ingredients:

- 2 eggs
- 2 lbs ground chicken breast
- 1/2 cup almond flour
- 1/2 cup ricotta cheese
- 1/4 cup fresh parsley, chopped
- 1 tsp pepper
- 2 tsp salt

Directions: Add all ingredients into the large bowl and mix until just combined. Make small balls from the meat mixture. Place the cooking tray in the air fryer basket. Line air fryer basket with parchment paper. Select Air Fry mode. Set time to 10 minutes and temperature 375 F then press START. The air fryer display will prompt you to ADD FOOD once the temperature is reached then place meatballs onto the parchment paper in the air fryer basket. Serve and enjoy.

Garlic Dip

Preparation time: 10 minutes cooking time: 20 minutes serve: 12

Ingredients:

- 3 garlic cloves, minced
- 5 oz Asiago cheese, shredded
- 1 cup sour cream
- 1 cup mozzarella cheese, shredded
- 8 oz cream cheese, softened

Directions:

Add all ingredients into the mixing bowl and mix until well combined. Pour mixture into the greased baking dish. Select Bake mode. Set time to 20 minutes and temperature 350 F then press START. The air fryer display will prompt you to ADD FOOD once the temperature is reached then place the baking dish in the air fryer basket. Serve and enjoy.

Crispy Zucchini Fries

Preparation time: 10 minutes cooking time: 20 minutes serve: 4

Ingredients:

- 2 eggs
- 2 medium zucchini, peel and cut into matchsticks
- 1/4 tsp onion powder
- 1 cup pork rinds, crushed
- 1 tbsp heavy cream
- 1/2 cup parmesan cheese, grated
- 1/4 tsp garlic powder

Directions:

In a bowl, whisk together cream and eggs. In a shallow dish, mix together crushed pork rinds, parmesan cheese, onion powder, and garlic powder. Dip each zucchini piece into the egg mixture then coat with pork rind mixture. Place the cooking tray in the air fryer basket. Line air fryer basket with parchment paper. Select Bake mode. Set time to 20 minutes and temperature 400 F then press START. The air fryer display will prompt you to ADD FOOD once the temperature is reached then place breaded zucchini fries onto the parchment paper in the air fryer basket. Serve and enjoy.

Cheesy Jalapeno Poppers

Preparation time: 10 minutes cooking time: 20 minutes serve: 24

Ingredients:

- 12 jalapeno peppers, cut in half and remove seeds
- 2 oz feta cheese
- 1/4 tsp garlic powder
- 1/2 tsp onion powder
- 1/4 cup cilantro, chopped
- 4 oz cheddar cheese, shredded
- 4 oz cream cheese

Directions: Add all ingredients except jalapeno peppers into the bowl and mix well to combine. Stuff cheese mixture into each jalapeno half. Place the cooking tray in the air fryer basket. Line air fryer basket with parchment paper. Select Bake mode. Set time to 20 minutes and temperature 400 F then press START. The air fryer display will prompt you to ADD FOOD once the temperature is reached then place jalapeno halves onto the parchment paper in the air fryer basket. Serve and enjoy

Roasted Cashew

Preparation time: 5 minutes cooking time: 10 minutes serve: 3

Ingredients:

- 3/4 cups cashews
- 1/2 tsp olive oil
- 1/2 tsp chili powder
- 1/4 tsp salt

Directions

Add all ingredients into the bowl and toss well. Place the cooking tray in the air fryer basket. Line air fryer basket with parchment paper. Select Bake mode. Set time to 10 minutes and temperature 250 F then press START. The air fryer display will prompt you to ADD FOOD once the temperature is reached then place cashews onto the parchment paper in the air fryer basket. Serve and enjoy.

Lamb Patties

Preparation time: 10 minutes cooking time: 8 minutes serve: 4

Ingredients:

- 1 lb ground lamb
- 1/4 cup fresh parsley, chopped
- 1 tsp dried oregano
- 1 cup feta cheese, crumbled
- 1 tbsp garlic, minced
- 5 basil leaves, minced
- 10 mint leaves, minced
- 1 jalapeno pepper, minced
- 1/4 tsp pepper
- 1/2 tsp kosher salt

Directions:

Add all ingredients into the mixing bowl and mix until well combined. Make four equal shape patties from the meat mixture. Place the cooking tray in the air fryer basket. Line air fryer basket with parchment paper. Select Bake mode. Set time to 8 minutes and temperature 390 F then press START. The air fryer display will prompt you to ADD FOOD once the temperature is reached then place patties onto the parchment paper in the air fryer basket. Serve and enjoy

Buffalo Chicken Dip

Preparation time: 10 minutes cooking time: 25 minutes serve: 8

Ingredients:

- 2 chicken breasts, skinless, boneless, cooked and shredded
- 1 cup Monterey jack cheese, shredded
- 1/2 cup ranch dressing
- 1/2 cup buffalo wing sauce
- 8 oz cream cheese, softened
- 1 cup cheddar cheese, shredded
- 1/4 cup blue cheese, crumbled

Directions:

Add cream cheese into the baking dish and top with shredded chicken, ranch dressing, and buffalo sauce. Sprinkle cheddar cheese, Monterey jack cheese, and blue cheese on top of chicken mixture. Cover dish with foil. Select Bake mode. Set time to 25 minutes and temperature 350 F then press START. The air fryer display will prompt you to ADD FOOD once the temperature is reached then place the baking dish in the air fryer basket. Serve and enjoy.

Ricotta Dip

Preparation time: 10 minutes cooking time: 15 minutes serve: 8

Ingredients:

- 1 cup ricotta cheese
- 1/2 tbsp fresh rosemary
- 1 tbsp lemon juice
- 2 tbsp olive oil
- 2 garlic cloves, minced
- 1/4 cup parmesan cheese
- 1/2 cup mozzarella cheese
- Pepper Salt

Directions:

Add ricotta cheese, garlic, oil, lemon juice, rosemary, pepper, and salt into the baking dish and mix until well combined. Sprinkle mozzarella cheese and parmesan cheese on top. Cover dish with foil. Select Bake mode. Set time to 15 minutes and temperature 400 F then press START. The air fryer display will prompt you to ADD FOOD once the temperature is reached then place the baking dish in the air fryer basket. Serve and enjoy.

Spicy Artichoke Dip

Preparation time: 10 minutes cooking time: 30 minutes serve: 12

Ingredients:

- 7 oz can green chiles, diced
- 15 oz can artichoke hearts, drained and chopped
- 2 cups mayonnaise
- 8 oz parmesan cheese, grated

Directions:

Add all ingredients into the mixing bowl and mix until well combined. Pour mixture into the 2-quart baking dish. Cover dish with foil. Select Bake mode. Set time to 30 minutes and temperature 325 F then press START. The air fryer display will prompt you to ADD FOOD once the temperature is reached then place the baking dish in the air fryer basket. Serve and enjoy.

Fresh Herb Mushrooms

Preparation time: 10 minutes cooking time: 14 minutes serve: 4

Ingredients:

- 1 lb mushrooms
- 1 tbsp basil, minced
- 1 garlic clove, minced
- 1/2 tbsp vinegar
- 1/2 tsp ground coriander
- 1 tsp rosemary, chopped Pepper Salt

Directions:

Add all ingredients into the large bowl and toss well. Place the cooking tray in the air fryer basket. Line air fryer basket with parchment paper. Select Bake mode. Set time to 14 minutes and temperature 350 F then press START. The air fryer display will prompt you to ADD FOOD once the temperature is reached then spread mushrooms onto the parchment paper in the air fryer basket. Serve and enjoy.

Zucchini Dill Dip

Preparation time: 10 minutes cooking time: 15 minutes serve: 6

Ingredients:

- 1 lb zucchini, grated & squeeze out all liquid
- 1 tsp garlic, minced
- 1 tsp dill, chopped
- 1 tbsp lime juice
- 1 tbsp olive oil
- 1 cup heavy cream
- Pepper Salt

Directions:

Add all ingredients into the large bowl and mix until well combined. Pour zucchini mixture into the prepared baking dish. Select Bake mode. Set time to 15 minutes and temperature 375 F then press START. The air fryer display will prompt you to ADD FOOD once the temperature is reached then place the baking dish in the air fryer basket. Serve and enjoy.

Cheddar Cheese Garlic Dip

Preparation time: 10 minutes cooking time: 8 minutes serve: 6

Ingredients:

- 13 oz cheddar cheese, remove the rind and cubed
- 3 garlic cloves, chopped
- 1 tbsp dried thyme
- 2 tsp rosemary, chopped
- Pepper Salt

Directions:

Add all ingredients into the mixing bowl and mix well. Pour mixture into the baking dish and cover dish with foil. Select Bake mode. Set time to 8 minutes and temperature 375 F then press START. The air fryer display will prompt you to ADD FOOD once the temperature is reached then place the baking dish in the air fryer basket. Serve and enjoy.

Air Fry Taro Fries

Preparation time: 10 minutes cooking time: 20 minutes serve: 2

Ingredients:

- 8 small taro, peel and cut into fries shape
- 1 tbsp olive oil
- 1/2 tsp chili powder
- 1/4 tsp garlic powder
- 1/4 tsp pepper
- 1/2 tsp salt

Directions:

Add taro fries in a bowl and drizzle with olive oil. Season with chili powder, garlic powder, pepper, and salt. Place the cooking tray in the air fryer basket. Line air fryer basket with parchment paper. Select Bake mode. Set time to 20 minutes and temperature 375 F then press START. The air fryer display will prompt you to ADD FOOD once the temperature is reached then place taro fries onto the parchment paper in the air fryer basket. Serve and enjoy.

Crispy Zucchini Chips

Preparation time: 10 minutes cooking time: 30 minutes serve: 2

Ingredients:

- 2 medium zucchini, cut into
- 1/4-inch thick slices
- 1/2 cup parmesan cheese, grated
- 1/4 cup olive oil
- Pepper Salt

Directions:

In a mixing bowl, toss zucchini slices with cheese, oil, pepper, and salt. Place the cooking tray in the air fryer basket. Line air fryer basket with parchment paper. Select Bake mode. Set time to 30 minutes and temperature 300 F then press START. The air fryer display will prompt you to ADD FOOD once the temperature is reached then arrange zucchini slices onto the parchment paper in the air fryer basket. Turn halfway through. Serve and enjoy.

Cinnamon Apple Chips

Preparation time: 10 minutes cooking time: 8 minutes serve: 4

Ingredients :

- 1 large apple, sliced thinly
- 1/4 tsp ground nutmeg
- 1/4 tsp ground cinnamon

Directions:

Season apple slices with nutmeg and cinnamon. Place the cooking tray in the air fryer basket. Line air fryer basket with parchment paper. Select Air Fry mode. Set time to 8 minutes and temperature 375 F then press START. The air fryer display will prompt you to ADD FOOD once the temperature is reached then place apple slices onto the parchment paper in the air fryer basket. Serve and enjoy.

Easy Sausage Balls

Preparation time: 10 minutes cooking time: 16 minutes serve: 10

Ingredients:

- 1 cup almond flour
- 1 lb ground sausage
- 1 cup cheddar cheese, shredded

Directions:

Add all ingredients into the mixing bowl and mix until well combined. Make 1-inch balls from meat mixture. Place the cooking tray in the air fryer basket. Place piece of aluminum foil into the air fryer basket. Select Air Fry mode. Set time to 16 minutes and temperature 375 F then press START. The air fryer display will prompt you to ADD FOOD once the temperature is reached then place meatballs onto the aluminum foil in the air fryer basket. Serve and enjoy.

Healthy Onion Rings

Preparation time: 10 minutes cooking time: 10 minutes serve: 3

Ingredients:

- 2 eggs, lightly beaten
- 2 large onions, peel & cut into
- 1-inch slices
- 1/2 tsp garlic powder
- 1 tsp paprika
- 2 tsp Italian seasoning
- 1 1/2 cups almond flour
- 1/2 tsp sea salt

Directions:

In a small bowl, add eggs and whisk well. In a shallow bowl, mix together almond flour, Italian seasoning, paprika, garlic powder, and sea salt. Dip onion slice into the egg then coat with almond flour mixture. Place breaded onion slices onto the parchment-lined plate and place it in the refrigerator for 30 minutes. Place the cooking tray in the air fryer basket. Place piece of parchment paper into the air fryer basket. Select Air Fry mode. Set time to 10 minutes and temperature 380 F then press START. The air fryer display will prompt you to ADD FOOD once the temperature is reached then place onion slices onto the parchment paper in the air fryer basket. Spray onion slices with cooking spray. Turn onion slices halfway through. Serve and enjoy.

Crispy Parmesan Asparagus Fries

Preparation time: 10 minutes cooking time: 12 minutes serve: 4

Ingredients:

- 3 eggs, lightly beaten
- 16 asparagus, trim 2-inches of bottom
- 1/2 cup parmesan cheese, grated
- 1 tbsp garlic powder
- 1/2 tbsp paprika
- 2 cups pork rinds, crushed
- 1 tbsp olive oil
- 2 tbsp heavy cream
- 1 tsp pepper

Directions: In a shallow dish, whisk eggs with olive oil, and heavy cream. On a plate, mix together crushed pork rinds, pepper, paprika, garlic powder, and parmesan cheese. Dip asparagus in egg then coat with pork rind mixture. Place the cooking tray in the air fryer basket. Place piece of parchment paper into the air fryer basket. Select Bake mode. Set time to 12 minutes and temperature 400 F then press START. The air fryer display will prompt you to ADD FOOD once the temperature is reached then place coated asparagus onto the parchment paper in the air fryer basket. Serve and enjoy

Crab Stuffed Jalapenos

Preparation time: 10 minutes cooking time: 20 minutes serve: 10

Ingredients:

- 8 oz lump crab meat
- 10 jalapenos, cut in half & remove seeds
- 2 green onions, sliced
- 3 bacon slices, cooked and crumbled
- 3/4 cup cheddar cheese, shredded
- 1/4 tsp garlic powder
- 1/2 tsp Cajun seasoning
- 4 oz cream cheese, softened

Directions: In a bowl, mix together crab meat, green onions, bacon, cheese, garlic powder, cajun seasoning, and cream cheese. Stuff crab meat mixture into each jalapeno half. Place the cooking tray in the air fryer basket. Select

Bake mode. Set time to 20 minutes and temperature 375 F then press START. The air fryer display will prompt you to ADD FOOD once the temperature is reached then place stuff jalapenos in the air fryer basket. Serve and enjoy.

Chicken Stuffed Poblanos

Preparation time: 10 minutes cooking time: 15 minutes serve: 6

Ingredients:

- 3 poblano pepper, cut in half & remove seeds
- 2 oz cheddar cheese, grated
- 1 1/2 cups spinach artichoke dip
- 1 cup chicken breast, cooked & chopped

Directions:

In a bowl, mix together chicken, spinach artichoke dip, and half cheddar cheese. Stuff chicken mixture into each poblano pepper half. Place the cooking tray in the air fryer basket. Line air fryer basket with parchment paper. Select Air Fry mode. Set time to 15 minutes and temperature 350 F then press START. The air fryer display will prompt you to ADD FOOD once the temperature is reached then place stuff poblano pepper onto the parchment paper in the air fryer basket. Sprinkle remaining cheese on top of stuff peppers. Serve and enjoy.

Thai Meatballs

Preparation time: 10 minutes cooking time: 20 minutes serve: 6

Ingredients:

- 2 eggs, lightly beaten
- 2 lbs ground turkey
- 1 tsp crushed red pepper
- 2 tbsp lemongrass, chopped
- 3 tbsp fish sauce
- 3 garlic cloves, minced
- 1/2 cup fresh basil, chopped
- 3/4 cup scallions, chopped
- 1 cup almond flour

Directions:

Add ground turkey in the mixing bowl. Add remaining ingredients and mix until well combined. Make small balls from the turkey mixture. Place the cooking tray in the air fryer basket. Line air fryer basket with parchment paper. Select Bake mode. Set time to 20 minutes and temperature 400 F then press START. The air fryer display will prompt you to ADD FOOD once the temperature is reached then place meatballs onto the parchment paper in the air fryer basket. Turn meatballs halfway through. Serve and enjoy.

Cheese Herb Zucchini

Preparation time: 10 minutes cooking time: 15 minutes serve: 4

Ingredients:

- 4 zucchini, quartered lengthwise
- 2 tbsp fresh parsley, chopped
- 1/2 tsp dried oregano
- 1/2 tsp dried thyme
- 1/2 cup parmesan cheese, grated
- 2 tbsp olive oil
- 1/4 tsp garlic powder
- 1/2 tsp dried basil
- Pepper Salt

Directions: In a small bowl, mix together parmesan cheese, garlic powder, basil, oregano, thyme, pepper, and salt. Place the cooking tray in the air fryer basket. Line air fryer basket with parchment paper. Select Bake mode. Set time to 15 minutes and temperature 350 F then press START. The air fryer display will prompt you to ADD FOOD once the temperature is reached then arrange zucchini onto the parchment paper in the air fryer basket. Drizzle with oil and sprinkle with parmesan cheese mixture. Garnish with parsley and serve.

Delicious Spinach Dip

Preparation time: 10 minutes cooking time: 20 minutes serve: 12

Ingredients:

- 3 oz frozen spinach, defrosted & chopped
- 1 cup cheddar cheese, shredded
- 8 oz cream cheese
- 1 cup Asiago cheese, shredded
- 1 cup sour cream
- 1 tsp salt

Directions:

Add all ingredients into the mixing bowl and mix until well combined. Transfer mixture into the baking dish. Cover dish with foil. Select bake mode. Set time to 20 minutes and temperature 350 f then press start. The air fryer display will prompt you to add food once the temperature is reached then baking dish in the air fryer basket. Serve and enjoy.

Mini Turkey and Corn Burritos

Prep + cook time: 25 minutes 6 servings

Ingredients

- 1 tablespoon olive oil
- ½ pound ground turkey
- 2 tablespoons shallot, minced
- 1 garlic clove, smashed 1 red bell pepper, seeded and chopped
- 1 ancho chili pepper, seeded and minced
- ½ teaspoon ground cumin
- Sea salt and freshly ground black pepper, to taste
- 1/3 cup salsa 6 ounces sweet corn kernels
- 12 8-inch tortilla shells 1 tablespoon butter, melted½ cup sour cream, for serving

Directions

Heat the olive oil in a sauté pan over medium-high heat. Cook the ground meat and shallots for 3 to 4 minutes. Add the garlic and peppers and cook an additional 3 minutes or until fragrant. After that, add the spices, salsa, and corn. Stir until everything is well combined. Place about 2 tablespoons of the meat mixture in the center of each tortilla. Roll your tortillas to seal the edges and make the burritos. Brush each burrito with melted butter and place them in the lightly greased cooking basket. Bake at 395 degrees F for 10 minutes, turning them over halfway through the cooking time. Garnish each burrito with a dollop of sour cream and serve.

Cheddar Cheese Lumpia Rolls

Prep + cook time: 20 minutes 5 servings

Ingredients

- 5 ounces mature cheddar cheese, cut into 15 sticks
- 15 pieces spring roll lumpia wrappers
- 2 tablespoons sesame oil

Directions

Wrap the cheese sticks in the lumpia wrappers. Transfer to the Air Fryer basket. Brush with sesame oil. Bake in the preheated Air Fryer at 395 degrees for 10 minutes or until the lumpia wrappers turn golden brown. Work in batches. Shake the Air Fryer basket occasionally to ensure even cooking. Enjoy!

Spicy Korean Short Ribs

Prep + cook time: 35 minutes 4 servings

Ingredients

- 1 pound meaty short ribs
- ½ rice vinegar
- ½ cup soy sauce
- 1 tablespoon brown sugar
- 1 tablespoons Sriracha sauce
- 2 garlic cloves, minced
- 1 tablespoon daenjang soybean paste
- 1 teaspoon kochukaru chili pepper flakes
- Sea salt and ground black pepper, to taste
- 1 tablespoon sesame oil
- ¼ cup green onions, roughly chopped

Directions

Place the short ribs, vinegar, soy sauce, sugar, Sriracha, garlic, and spices in Ziploc bag; let it marinate overnight. Rub the sides and bottom of the Air Fryer basket with sesame oil. Discard the marinade and transfer the ribs to the prepared cooking basket. Cook the marinated ribs in the preheated Air Fryer at 365 degrees for 17 minutes. Turn the ribs over, brush with the reserved marinade, and cook an additional 15 minutes. Garnish with green onions. Serve and enjoy!

Crunchy Asparagus with Mediterranean Aioli

Prep + cook time: 50 minutes 4 servings

Ingredients

Crunchy Asparagus:

- 2 eggs
- ¾ cup breadcrumbs
- 2 tablespoons Parmesan cheese
- Sea salt and ground white pepper, to taste
- ½ pound asparagus, cleaned and trimmed
- Cooking spray

Mediterranean Aioli:

- 4 garlic cloves, minced
- 4 tablespoons olive oil
- mayonnaise 1 tablespoons
- lemon juice, freshly squeezed

Directions

Start by preheating your Air Fryer to 400 degrees F. In a shallow bowl, thoroughly combine the eggs, breadcrumbs, Parmesan cheese, salt, and white pepper. Dip the asparagus spears in the egg mixture; roll to coat well. Cook in the preheated Air Fryer for 5 to 6 minutes; work in two batches. Place the garlic on a piece of aluminum foil and spritz with cooking spray. Wrap the garlic in the foil. Cook in the preheated Air Fryer at 400 degrees for 12 minutes. Check the garlic, open the top of the foil and continue to cook for 10 minutes more. Let it cool for 10 to 15 minutes; remove the cloves by squeezing them out of the skins; mash the garlic and add the mayo and fresh lemon juice; whisk until everything is well combined. Serve the asparagus with the chilled aioli on the side. Enjoy!

Cheesy Zucchini Sticks

Prep + cook time: 20 minutes 2 servings

Ingredients

- 1 zucchini, slice into strips
- 2 tablespoons mayonnaise
- ¼ cup tortilla chips, crushed
- ¼ cup Romano cheese, shredded
- Sea salt and black pepper, to your liking
- 1 tablespoon garlic powder
- ½ teaspoon red pepper flakes

DIRECTIONS Coat the zucchini with mayonnaise. Mix the crushed tortilla chips, cheese and spices in a shallow dish. Then, coat the zucchini sticks with the cheese/chips mixture. Cook in the preheated Air Fryer at 400 degrees F for 12 minutes, shaking the basket halfway through the cooking time. Work in batches until the sticks are crispy and golden brown. Serve and enjoy!

Parsnip Chips with Spicy Citrus Aioli

Prep + cook time: 20 minutes 4 servings

Ingredients

- 1 pound parsnips, peel long strips
- 2 tablespoons sesame oil
- Sea salt and ground black pepper, to taste
- 1 teaspoon red pepper flakes, crushed
- ½ teaspoon curry powder
- ½ teaspoon mustard seeds

Spicy Citrus Aioli:

- ¼ cup mayonnaise
- 1 tablespoon fresh lime juice
- 1 clove garlic, smashed

- Salt and black pepper, to taste

DIRECTIONS Start by preheating the Air Fryer to 380 degrees F. Toss the parsnip chips with the sesame oil, salt, black pepper, red pepper, curry powder, and mustard seeds. Cook for 15 minutes, shaking the Air Fryer basket periodically. Meanwhile, make the sauce by whisking the mayonnaise, lime juice, garlic, salt, and pepper. Place in the refrigerator until ready to use. Enjoy!

Bacon Chips with Chipotle Dipping Sauce

Prep + cook time: 15 minutes 3 servings

Ingredients

- 6 ounces bacon, cut into strips

Chipotle Dipping Sauce:

- 6 tablespoons sour cream
- ½ teaspoon chipotle
- chili powder

Directions

Place the bacon strips in the Air Fryer cooking basket. Cook the bacon strips at 360 degrees F for 5 minutes; turn them over and cook for another 5 minutes. Meanwhile, make the chipotle dipping sauce by whisking the sour cream and chipotle chili powder; reserve. Serve the bacon chips with the chipotle dipping sauce and enjoy!

Fish Sticks with Honey Mustard Sauce

Prep + cook time: 10 minutes 3 servings

Ingredients

- 10 ounces fish sticks
- ½ cup mayonnaise
- 2 teaspoons yellow mustard
- 2 teaspoons honey

Directions

Add the fish sticks to the Air Fryer cooking basket; drizzle the fish sticks with a nonstick cooking spray. Cook the fish sticks at 400 degrees F for 5 minutes; turn them over and cook for another 5 minutes. Meanwhile, mix the mayonnaise, yellow mustard and honey until well combined. Serve the fish sticks with the honey mustard sauce for dipping. Enjoy!

<u>THANK YOU</u>

Thank you for choosing *Quick & Easy Recipes for Appetizers* for improving your cooking skills! I hope you enjoyed making the recipes as much as tasting them! If you're interested in learning new recipes and new meals to cook, go and check out the other books of the series.

Lightning Source UK Ltd.
Milton Keynes UK
UKHW021841040521
383144UK00003B/448